A Field Where Memories Grow

Vol. 2 of Short Stories & Poetry

Mary Joyce Lawhorn

A Field Where Memories Grow
Copyright©2012 By: Mary Joyce Lawhorn

All rights reserved. No part of this book may be reproduced in any form by any electronic or mechanical means including photocopying, recording, or information storage and retrieval without permission in writing from the author.

This is a work of fiction.
Any similarities to persons living or dead are purely coincidental.

Contributing cover photo by: Tina Turner

ISBN-10: 0988292629
ISBN-13: 978-0-9882926-2-8

The Seashell Books
www.theseashellbooks.com
Email: seashellbooks@gmail.com

Table of Contents

Page 1 . . . . . . Memories
Page 2 . . . . . . Wishing Well
Page 3 . . . . . . Battle of the Milky Way
Page 4 . . . . . . A Field Where Memories Grow
Page 5 . . . . . . The Things I See
Page 6 . . . . . . The Red Slippers
Page 15 . . . . . Diamond Dan
Page 23 . . . . . Stolen Youth
Page 24 . . . . . Lazy Daisy
Page 27 . . . . . A Mother's Heartstrings
Page 29 . . . . . Angels Among Us
Page 34 . . . . . Getting Old
Page 35 . . . . . Dream Traveler
Page 37 . . . . . I Am Not a Rat!
Page 44 . . . . . Green Apples for Big Red
Page 47 . . . . . True Love
Page 48 . . . . . It's Hot Outside
Page 49 . . . . . Pesky Pest
Page 50 . . . . . Nature's Music
Page 51 . . . . . Are You Asleep Momma?
Page 54 . . . . . Abby's Two Worlds
Page 58 . . . . . Where All Good People Go
Page 60 . . . . . Another Sound
Page 61 . . . . . Rain Storms

Page 62 . . . . . Grandma
Page 63 . . . . . One Lion's Secret
Page 64 . . . . . Hearts
Page 65 . . . . . Changes
Page 66 . . . . . A Visit
Page 67 . . . . . Losing Game
Page 68 . . . . . Mother's Day
Page 69 . . . . . Rat Race
Page 74 . . . . . Taken for Granted
Page 75 . . . . . Paradise Lost
Page 76 . . . . . Homeless
Page 77 . . . . . A Spider's Web
Page 78 . . . . . Mr. Owl & Mr. Bat
Page 79 . . . . . The Wonder of Life
Page 80 . . . . . Snow Covered Creek
Page 81 . . . . . Another Shadow
Page 82 . . . . . The Old Barn
Page 84 . . . . . A Tree's Life
Page 85 . . . . . A Happy Place
Page 86 . . . . . Only One Shoe
Page 88 . . . . . Tea Cup
Page 89 . . . . . Trusting Heart
Page 90 . . . . . Don't Let it Grow
Page 91 . . . . . Bugs, Slugs & Butterflies
Page 92 . . . . . Angry Storm
Page 93 . . . . . Old House
Page 95 . . . . . Her First Day of School
Page 96 . . . . . When Men Were Free

Page 97 . . . . . Just the Way You Are
Page 98 . . . . . Bad Seed
Page 100 . . . . My Empty Heart
Page 101 . . . . A Battle Won
Page 102 . . . . Memories in a Bottle
Page 103 . . . . In Time
Page 104 . . . . Old Poets Never Die

Mary Joyce Lawhorn

Memories

*I have my memories
of days gone by,
Most are happy,
some make me cry.*

*I see you now
when you were small,
With little hands
catching a ball.*

*Standing at my door
with a big surprise,
A box so shiny,
as bright as your eyes.*

*A cup of memories
of when you were a little boy,
And how you filled
my life with joy.*

*You were the first
of five to come along,
Then a little girl
we were blessed to bring home.*

Wishing Well

A little boy and his wishing well,
Making his wishes and wouldn't tell.

If I tell they won't come true!
So nanny he said, I can't even tell you.

Years went by and the well went dry,
But the pennies reached up to the sky.

Still he came by and lay his penny down,
Making a wish while looking around.

You know nanny, I love coming here,
He told her with a hint of a tear.

I am sorry son your wishes didn't come true,
If I could I would have granted them to you.

Oh! But nanny I thought you knew!
It was only an excuse to come see you.

Mary Joyce Lawhorn

Battle of the Milky Way

I go for weeks without a snack,
Losing weight just to gain it back.
For a while I'm slim and lean,
No fat rolling over my jean.
Then a Milky Way bar starts calling me,
I devour it down with a cup of tea.
Just one won't hurt I rationalize,
After all it was the mini size.
But the graving grew more than I thought,
Another battle lost that I had fought.
The Milky Way won again this time,
Feeding on this craving of mine.
Now my jeans don't fit me anymore,
I'm ready for battle against the candy store.
I will win the battle but not the war,
As I did so many times before.

A Field
Where Memories Grow

A field of memories
as far as the eye can see,
Where I walk
with my memories and me.

My field is where
only loved ones can go,
Where seeds were planted
and I watched them grow.

Only good memories
in my field will abound,
For the bad ones are hidden
deep under the ground.

Where thistles grow
and the earth is clay
In another field
that's far- far and away.

Mary Joyce Lawhorn

The Things I See

I know this has
often been said,
"I wish I could express
what's in my head."

But words won't come
and inside they stay,
So I can't say
what I want to say.

I try to describe
everything around,
And to write a meaning
to every sound.

But the world is too big
and full of mystery,
To try and describe
all the things I see.

The Red Slippers

The words blared from the front page of the *Grandville Daily*.

Local family savagely murdered; their thirteen year old daughter missing!

By the time the paper was printed, the townspeople had already heard about the Walker family demise. Every door was locked, drapes were drawn and no one went out after dark. Very few ventured out during the day. Nothing this awful had ever happened in Grandville, Ohio.

Like most small towns everyone knew each other, and the Walkers were no exception. They were known to be a hardworking, honest family that went to church every Sunday and always there when a neighbor was sick or needed help. It didn't make sense that something this bad could happen to them.

Little Ann was only three years old, her brother was seven and Martha was thirteen. Mr. Walker had worked on his farm along with his wife for twenty years and everything they owned came directly or indirectly from that little piece of land they had bought when they first moved to Grandville as newlyweds.

The funeral was the sadist thing the town had ever witnessed. Even worse, Martha Walker was still missing. Not a trace of her was found in the weeks they combed the fields and woods searching for any clue as to what had become of her.

A few of the men in town looked all over the house the morning after the murders had taken place. Martha's bed looked as if it hadn't been slept in. Even her red slippers were neatly tucked under her bed. In the corner, hung a line of dresses that Mrs. Walker had made her daughter from flour sacks. The odd thing to everyone was Martha's room was the only room in the house that was not saturated with blood.

A year passed and then another. Even after sixteen years, no family had occupied the Walker house. It seemed no one in town wanted to live in a place where such evil had taken place. Weeds had taken over the yard that once was so beautiful, it could have been a picture post card. The fields that used to produce bountiful crops of corn were now brown and overgrown with weeds and thistles. The house was in dire need of repair, with broken windows and paint peeling off.

Time passed and the tragedy was still talked about from time to time, but little Martha Walker was never far from the minds of people that remembered that day. They wondered where she was. Some thought she may still be alive, while others wished her body could be found so that she could be laid to rest with the rest of her family.

It wasn't too long before folks started to let down their guard, where again doors were left ajar during the hot summer nights and children played out in their backyards until after dark. Things were beginning to get back to normal. Even the Walker farm was sold to a family who would be moving there soon.

Being the good neighbors everyone was in Grandville, they decided to mow down the weeds and white wash the old house. Some of the women volunteered to clean the inside of the house, but they were warned about how gruesome it might be in some of the rooms. They had no idea what they would find. The first room they entered was the dining area that adjoined the kitchen. The women were shocked to see how clean the all the rooms were. It was as if time had stood still inside the house while the outside withered and faded.

No one had any way of knowing that there was someone still living in the house - maybe not in body, but spirit.

Martha heard the women talking downstairs and ran to see who was there. She thought some neighbors had come to visit her mother, but her mother wasn't among them. She recognized Mable Crowe and Liz Brown, even though they had changed. They looked older to her.

The women stood around with confused expressions on their faces as they examined the china in the cabinets. Then they checked inside the refrigerator and the pantry while Martha walked around them without even being noticed. She tried to get Mrs. Crows attention by pulling on her apron strings, but Mrs. Crowe shivered and tied it back. She was the first of the women to suggest to the others that they should go.

It seemed to Martha that the women were a little on edge about being there. Martha wondered where her family was, and why all these women were in her house.

Martha was awakened from sleep by the sound of her mother cooking breakfast. She even smelled biscuits baking. She jumped out of bed and into her red slippers then ran to the stairs. She could see from there the kitchen was empty and no one was cooking. She must have been dreaming or maybe it was a flashback from another time. She didn't know.

The girl wasn't hungry anyway. She hadn't been hungry or thirsty for a long time. She really didn't need anything because she didn't feel her own body. She knew that when she stepped on the cold floor, she didn't feel the cold on her bare feet like she once did. It was always cold back then in the winter time. Now, it was as if her body had gone somewhere and left her spirit behind. She remembered her family and her life in this house, though she didn't remember what had happened to them or her. Martha didn't know she was murdered along with her family.

She couldn't comprehend time either. It was as if she went to sleep one night and woke up the next morning to the sound of Mable Crowe and the other women in her mother's kitchen.

Martha stayed in her room most of the time after that. She was in a place of nonexistence-sleeping-nothing. All she knew was when she found herself back in the house, she always felt refreshed and rested. She was there for a reason. She knew that without a doubt. It was a sense she had - a mission so to speak.

✧ ✧ ✧

Again Martha heard a familiar sound of someone in the kitchen banging pots and pans, so she slipped in her red slippers and went to the top of the stairs. This time it was real, for she saw a young woman bent over putting bread in the oven. For a split second she thought it was her mother.

There was a girl about Martha's age sitting at the dining room table reading a paper. To Martha she was dressed a little strange. To get a closer look, she slipped down the long stairs until she was on the bottom step without the woman even noticing. But the girl looked up as if she heard something and looked straight at the spot where Martha stood, but then went back to her reading.

Jenny had seen the red slippers on the bottom step, and she knew they were not alone. She knew that sooner or later the spirit would return, for she knew they were all on a mission.

"Honey, breakfast is ready! And please hurry because you don't want to be late on your first day at school."

Martha was close enough now to see what the girl was reading, and she could see it was yellow from age.

"Mama, you have got to see something in this old paper!" Jenny said excitedly.

"Jenny, I will read it later, but you need to scoot." The mother lovingly said as she swatted her daughter across the butt as she ran out the door.

The paper was dated Saturday, September 12th 1910. Martha was wondering why it was so old looking.

The woman picked up the paper before Martha could read anything else. She had gone over to pour herself another cup of coffee, and then went back with her dainty little cup to continued reading something she seemed to be pretty engrossed in. Martha was looking over the mother's shoulder and reading the paper too. There on the front page was a school photo of the children she went to school with, though varying in ages. She remembered keeping that particular issue in her room for years. In fact, since the second grade, because it was the first time a photographer ever traveled to the one room school to make a group picture of the students for the local paper.

Martha knew every word by heart in that paper, so she looked around the kitchen. That's when she became aware the people who had moved in had changed almost everything. On the wall to her right was a calendar. It was different from the ones she had seen before. This one had a painting of a beautiful girl wearing a huge hat and drinking a cola, dated January, 1965.

That can't be! Martha thought. That would make me fifty two. I am only thirteen! She ran to the mirror, but as hard as she tried, she couldn't see her reflection. She felt fifteen, not fifty two. Besides that, she could still wear her red slippers.

+ + +

Little by little things started to fall into place for Martha. She knew now she was there on a mission - a mission to find her own body. All she had to do now was to try to remember where she was on the last day she was alive. She was going to need help, and she thought of Jenny, the young girl who lived there now; the one who had all of her things in Martha's old room.

As Jenny rushed around the house after she came home from school, Martha was there beside her, trying with all her might to get the girl to notice her. There were times Jenny would stop suddenly and look in Martha's direction. This went on for days before Martha realized something. It's the slippers! Jenny can see only my slippers!

Then one evening, Jenny was sitting on her bed when out of the corner of her eye she saw the red slippers move. "Martha, is that you?" she asked in a whisper.

"Yes, it's me! Jenny, I am right in front of you. Look at my feet!" Martha pushed the pillow to the floor where her feet were.

"What are you here for?" Jenny asked aloud. She couldn't hear Martha speak, but she felt her presence. "If it has something to do with what happened to your family, move the pillow again." Jenny said as she picked the pillow up and placed it back on the bed.

The pillow moved in rapid succession from one side of the bed to the other.

"Are you lost or separated from your family?"

The pillow moved again.

"Martha, when I ask you a question, could you move the pillow once for yes and twice for no?"

The pillow moved once.

"Do you want me to find out what happened to your family?"

The pillow moved twice.

"That's not it…have you come here to find something?"

Again the pillow moved once for yes.

Jenny wasn't frightened of the girl who was there with her, for she had experienced this before. It all started when she was five, and her parents had taken her to all sorts of doctors. But they all assured them that it wasn't uncommon for children to have make-believe-friends. She would outgrow it. But Jenny never out grew her gift to communicate with the dead, though she never confided in her parents about all the friends from the spirit world she had made over the years.

✦✦✦

Each day when Jenny returned home from school, she would rush to her room to be with her friend, Martha who was always there waiting.

"I think I know what you are here for." Jenny said where Martha could hear her. "You are looking for your body, aren't you?" The pillow moved once.

"Do you remember where you were when you died?" No was the signal.

"I am going to do some research and we are going to find your body." Jenny felt something warm encircle her body as if someone had hugged her. She knew it was her friend.

Everything Jenny could find out about the Walker murders she would write it down in her notebook. She talked to the older people in town, but most of what she got was handed down by word of mouth, which she felt was as close to the truth as it could be after so many years had gone by. She did know the girl's body was never found.

Jenny learned where the men had searched, that being mostly in the woods and fields. No one mentioned anyplace close to the house, not even the dug well behind the house. No one mentioned that could be Martha's grave.

Although it was covered and nailed down, it could have been like that even before the family was murdered, but it gave Jenny an uneasy feeling just looking at it, let alone go near it. That is why she had asked her father several times when he was going to fill it in. He was planning on it later, but he couldn't understand why his daughter was in such a hurry, and Jenny didn't know either. Her father figured his warning to her about the danger of the well had scared her more than he had meant to.

✦ ✦ ✦

Jenny came home to find a group of men gathered around the well, and she could see where the walls had been torn down and the wood slab on top had been pulled off. Her father saw her coming and rushed to meet her so he could stop her from seeing what they had discovered in the deep hole.

"You found Martha's bones didn't you daddy?" Jenny asked, but she really wasn't sure she wanted to know.

"How do you know that, Jenny?" But he knew all along his daughter's gift had never gone away.

"Go in the house and stay with your mother. I will be in later."

Jenny went to her room instead. "Martha," she called.

"I am here, Jenny. They found my body didn't they?" she said, knowing Jenny couldn't hear her.

"Martha, I know you are here. Please move the pillow if you know they have found your body." The pillow moved once.

Jenny knew Martha would be leaving soon, for that's what happened to all her friends when their mission was over. But this friend was different than all the other ones that she had made over the years. She was going to miss her now that her search was over.

"Goodbye, Martha, I will see you again one day." Jenny said and Martha signaled once.

At that very moment a stream of tears fell to the floor and landed on top of the red slippers that Martha was wearing.

A few days later, Jenny went to her room. It seemed lonely to her since her friend had left, but this day was different. She knew Martha had been there, for on her bed next to a pillow was Martha's red slippers.

The End

DIAMOND DAN

Diamond Dan lived in a huge house. His family was very wealthy and so afraid someone might rob them, that they rarely left the house that was full of diamonds and fine gems. So the situation was Diamond Dan had few friends when he was small. The only folks he ever saw were the delivery men and maybe the postman, if he was up early enough. Other than on those occasions, he didn't see anyone at all.

Diamond Dan didn't understand why he could not go out to play with the other little gems in his neighborhood; then when he turned ten, he was allowed to go play with his close neighbors, but he wasn't allowed to go to his friends' houses that lived further away. They could only come to his house. Why, Pearl, lived just up the street from him and they used to have lots of fun when she came over, but she didn't want to play with Dan anymore and would hardly even speak to him if she saw him looking out the window. Dan thought Pearl was a little on the sensitive side. He thought it was because she was only a pearl and not a precious diamond such as himself, was the reason she shied away from him.

"Why everyone knows diamonds are worth more than pearls!" He thought to himself, but he couldn't help but remember how sad little Pearl looked when he told her so. Diamond Dan had a lot to learn as to how he should treat the other gems.

Pearl never invited Diamond Dan over to play again and he missed her, especially when he could see from his bedroom window how much fun she and the other little gem friends were having. He would watch at a distance when beautiful Pearl was outside with her friend, Emerald Emily, a little gem he met once at a party. As he watched them having fun, Diamond Dan became very sad and wondered why Pearl would prefer Emerald's company over his. "I am a precious diamond and she is a mere emerald!" he cried, and as tears ran down his face the sparkle and shine seemed to wash away with his tears. Now, if he was put side to side with plain glass, you wouldn't be able to tell the difference. Diamond Dan had not yet learned how precious all gems are. He thought because he was so protected, that he was better than they were.

Diamond Dan fell ill that day, and he was so pale, the sparkle he once had was now a dull, flat look. His mother tried to console him, but it was no use. No matter what mother Diamond did, she could not coax him out of his bed.

So Dan's mother invited some of her garden friends little gems over, thinking if he saw how sparkly and shiny they were, it would encourage Diamond Dan to get out of bed and become himself again. When the diamond gems came into little Dan's bedroom, he was all covered up because he didn't want them to be seen or bothered by them. "Just go away, I am ill and don't feel like playing today." He moaned.

"Oh nonsense!" they replied. "Diamonds are tough. After all, we are the most precious gems."

And with that, they pulled the cover off of Diamond Dan's head. In shocked union they all shouted, "You're not Diamond Dan, you are only a common piece of glass.

We can't play with you!" with that they ran out of Dan's room.

"Of course, I am Diamond Dan!" he shouted after them. He thought, *I am still the same inside. I may look different but I am the same gem I have always been.*

Mother Diamond heard him crying and rushed to his room. She knew why the little diamonds had left, and it reminded her of a time when she was a little gem. She sat down beside her son and put her arms around him.

"I don't want to be a diamond anymore!" he cried. "No one likes me. I want to be a pearl or an emerald because they have more friends than diamonds."

Mother Diamond said to Dan, "Let me tell you a story. It was a long time ago when I was just about your age." She went on to tell him about the days she grew up in what most considered the wealthiest family of all the precious gems. "In those days, my mother was very beautiful, and she was a very rare gem — a blue diamond— and because of this she had to live a very sheltered life as well. I was born a white diamond, but as it was, I had to live a sheltered life like my mother did. And there was no such thing as our associating with anyone other than the diamond family. One day I was walking in the garden and came upon a stone. I thought it was a stone for I had never seen anything like it. It was just lying there before me in the dirt, all dirty. But I could see a glimmer of gold peeping through the dirt when the sun hit it just right. "

"My name is Diamond Tierra," I introduced myself. "What is your name?" I asked.

"Oh please, Miss Diamond, you should not be out here talking to me! I am but a small piece of gold someone lost a long time ago."

"You must get very cold and lonely out here. I will take you inside and the maids will make you all shiny again. And my parents may let you stay with us."

"No, that would be unthinkable!" he whispered. "I know your family, and I have seen the gems that come and go here. They are all like you, Miss Diamond, so beautiful and full of shinning brilliance. I couldn't possibly present my lowly self to your family. Please go away before your mother misses you and finds you out here with me."

"It made me sad to leave the gold stone out in the garden all alone, but he was so stubborn and proud and he insisted I do so."

"Please, before I go, would you tell me your name?" I asked.

"I guess it would be ok. But don't laugh! It is Gold Ring."

He paused, waiting for the beautiful diamond to poke fun at his unusual name. But to the contrary," she replied.

"That is a nice name. Someone must have loved you very much to have given you such a beautiful name. May I come to visit you again when I am allowed to come out to the garden?" Diamond smiled.

"You must never see me again, Miss Diamond. If you were seen with me, you would never be allowed to come out here again, and I suffer to think what would become of me."

"With that, I never saw Gold Ring again — that is until years later. I was about to turn sixteen and my parents were planning a huge birthday party for me. Things had changed somewhat over the years, and I was allowed to socialize with the rubies, the emeralds, the pearls and a few others from the gold families, but only if they were wealthy and accepted in the social circles."

Mother Diamond felt sad about it, but that is the way it was and is in some gem circles. Mother Diamond continued on telling her story to Dan.

"As time drew near to my party, I was so excited. But there was always a little sadness that would not go away. My mind would wander back to the time I had met the Golden Ring and how I would for weeks return to the garden looking for him. Then weeks turned into years, and I thought I would never see him again."

Now the day of my party had arrived. My friends, the rubies, the pearls, and the diamonds all arrived on time. Then about an hour into the party, the doorbell rang. When I opened the door, there stood the most handsome, gold solder, all decorated in the shiniest gold armor I had ever seen.

"May I come in, Miss Diamond?" he asked and he bent down and kissed her on the hand.

"Gold Ring, I would know your voice anywhere!" Diamond Tierra screamed. "Where have you been? I came searching for you every day."

"I am sorry, Tierra, I saw you and it was all I could do to keep from answering you, but I knew the danger I would be in if someone saw you with such a lowly thing as me, not to mention depriving myself of a glimpse of your beauty, at least I could look upon you from afar."

"You were in the garden all the time! I should never have stopped looking for you." Tears came to Mother Diamond's eyes as she told Dan the story, just as they did that day so long ago.

"Please don't cry, Miss Diamond. I wasn't there all those years. One day late in the spring, your Gardner found me and being the honest man he was, he took me to your parents. They told him I was only a piece of dirty stone and for him to keep it. The Gardner took me home with him and cleaned me up until I was as shiny as new gold. I had to be worth something. The Gardner was very poor and had to sell me. That's how I ended up being sold to a family with a long line of royalty. They took me in, and I became a part of their family. I knew someday I would come back here when I was worthy of you and more presentable." He smiled.

"By this time, all the party guests were standing around Tierra and Gold Ring. Some were whispering among themselves, others were staring in amazement, wondering who this tall, good looking gold solder was and just how Tierra had come to make his acquaintance. After all, they all knew each other in their circle of friends and no one had ever seen him before."

Mother Diamond paused a second from her story, reflecting back to that time. Little Diamond Dan wanted her to hurry and get back to the story.

"Please, Mother, tell me, who was the Gold Solder, and where did he go?"

Mother diamond came back to the present and saw Dan had some of the sparkle back in his face, insisting she tell him the rest of her story.

"Well, since you are looking so much better, I guess I can tell you what happened next."

Little Diamond had never seen his mother shine as bright as she did at that moment.

"The Gold Solder is your father, and he asked me to marry him that day. We were married a short time later, right in the beautiful garden where we had first met. Even though a lot of my friends thought I should have married a diamond, most were very happy for us. There was one thing they all could agree on and that was we were the finest looking couple any of them had ever seen. Your father wore his gold armor. He was so proud and tall with his new wife on his arm. So you see, Dan, if I had walked on by the gold stone, and not noticed the gold color shining through the dirt, I may never have met your father. And it is the same with all things. We have to look inside and sometimes when we do, we can find the most beautiful things. For example, your friend Pearl, before she was born, she was in a plain brown shell. No one could imagine that a beautiful white pearl lay inside waiting for someone to find her. Do you understand what I am saying Dan?"

"I think so. Was I found in a brown shell mother?"

"No son, but that is the beauty of us all being different. We may all come from all sorts of backgrounds, like Pearl came from a plain brown shell. You, though, came from a huge mountain which was a diamond mine, among rocks and soil."

"Like my dad?" Dan asked.

"Yes," answered his mother. "Just like your father whom was very proud to have been born in the gold family and never thought he was better than any of the other gems that may have been less fortunate than he was. I was a diamond and he thought I was beautiful." Mother Diamond blushed. "But remember…" his mother continued, "…he never did want to be a diamond himself or any other fine gem. He wants you to be proud of what you are, but no better than any of your friends, because try as we may, we can't change what we are. We cannot take a white pearl and make it a black pearl, although a black pearl is worth more materially, same as we cannot turn a white diamond into a blue diamond, which is far more rare than a white diamond. We are all what is in the eye of the beholder, which is why, to your father and I, you are the most precious of all gems, just as little Pearl and Emerald Emily are to their parents.

Diamond Dan understood better now as to why he was so protected, but he had though it was because he was better than his friends, which only made him lonely and sad.

All the sparkle had returned to Dan's face, and he was himself again. He jumped out of bed and this made his mother happy, and she agreed with Dan that he should have a block party and invite all the little gems to come. He made a list of the gems he would invite; little Pearl down the street, Emily Emerald and there was Ruby Red, whom he hadn't seen in a long time. Maybe Jade Green would come and Opal White. She had such a good sense of humor. This would be the best party ever if everyone came. There was so much to talk about and so much to learn from his many gem and precious metal and mineral neighbors. He sent many invitations out and the list went on and on….Copper Kittle, Crystal Clear, Lead Pencil, Yellow and White Gold who were twins. Silver Spoon, Garnet Black, Amber Bright, Cora Coral, Moon stone, Jay Jadeite and a cousin he had never met, little Blue Diamond. He thought about the little Diamond friend that ran away from him because he seemed to be plain glass; he would invite them because like himself, they could learn a few things too, so he sent them all an invitation to his party.

The End

Mary Joyce Lawhorn

Stolen Youth

Before she knew it, she was alone,
The house was empty, the children gone.
It got harder to find something to do,
For getting old takes its toll on you.

She went to the window and looked outside,
The sun was shining but she still cried.
It seems as if it was yesterday,
Her world was perfect, she was okay.

No worries to keep her awake at night,
And all her troubles were out of sight.
She never dreamed what was to come,
Her happiness was numbered under the sun.
The clouds gathered and darkened the day,
Then stole her youth and walked away.

Lazy Daisy

There was a lady
they called Lazy Daisy.
She was dirty they say,
and really lazy.

Her grass grew high
up to the door,
Even the cat
wouldn't eat off her floor.

She lived on
water and bread,
And even her cat
was rarely fed.

Then one day
her cat went missing,
No more meowing
and no more hissing.

He found a home
just over the hill,
Where food was plenty
and got his fill.

Mary Joyce Lawhorn

He never missed
Lazy Daisy at all,
Even though his name
she would often call.

It would echo through the canyon
both night and day,
Come here kitty,
come home right away!

She didn't blame her cat
for not coming home,
There was nothing in her cupboard
but a dried up bone.

Not even enough
to make some stew,
Now Lazy Daisy knew
what she would do.

She got on her bike
and rode into town,
Got a loaf of bread
and a big juicy ham.

She bought a batch
of fresh caught fish,
To put in her cat's
favorite dish.

A Field Were Memories Grow

Now kitty will come home,
she thought,
After he sees
what all I've bought.

Come home kitty,
come home she cried,
You have fish
and a big ham I fried.

But little kitty was full
and fast asleep,
And from under his bed
he didn't even peek.

A Mothers Heartstring's

A mother of four was preparing to go into the hospital to have a hysterectomy in three weeks. When the time came for her surgery, she was very nervous and thought she might die while undergoing her surgical procedure.

She thought of her children and couldn't stand the thought of not being there for them because they were all young. For some reason, she had flashes in her mind of headlines in the paper:

Young mother dies undergoing a simple operation

The nurses had prepped the woman, and she had been given a sedative. Her husband was with her when she told him she had changed her mind about having a hysterectomy and wanted to go home. The husband thought the sedative had caused his wife to panic, and he rushed out of the room to get a nurse.

Her Doctor came in to assure her that he had performed this procedure many times, and she had nothing to worry about. With a third degree prolapsed uterus, she needed to have this done. After a few more words of encouragement, and a pat on her shoulder, he left the room.

Meanwhile, all was well as far as everyone thought. When the nurse came to roll her into surgery, the bed was empty and the husband had stepped out for a second. When her husband came back in, the nurse asked him where his wife was, but he didn't know. "She was there just a minute ago!" he told her.

The hospital staff was panicking, for they had lost a patient and the doctor was in the operating room waiting.

One of the nurses found the young woman in the lobby, and asked her how in the world she had gotten down to the first floor as heavily sedated as she was.

However, she was determined to go home, and needless to say, she slept all the way home, happy that she would see her children.

After a few weeks, she realized how bad she was getting and that she could hemorrhage to death. This time she couldn't back out. After all, she had her children to think about. An appointment was made with her doctor to reschedule.

At the office, she told her doctor that he needed to do a pregnancy test on her for she had misses her period. After a while, the test came back that she was about six weeks pregnant.

Her doctor couldn't believe it and told her if she had not backed out that day at the hospital, there would have been no way of knowing until her uterus was removed and examined that she was two weeks along.

Were those microscopic little hands tugging at his mother's heartstring?

I believe they were, and do for a mother's lifetime.

Angels Among Us

During my childhood, we were taught that each of us had a guarding angel watching over us. Remembering the following stories rekindled that childhood belief.

Elizabeth's angel was there guiding her throughout her childhood years, but as she grew into her pre-teen, she believed her angel went on to help someone else who needed her more. The absence of her angel wasn't immediately known to Elizabeth. It wasn't as if she had this premonition or something, she just never got those feelings she would have as a child. Had her angel really left her, or had she left her angel? Elizabeth's near-death experience proved the latter.

It was Elizabeth's thirteenth birthday, and her mother had asked her to go to the store for her. The family didn't own a car in those days. So Elizabeth was used to walking, either alone or her mother would go with her when she needed more than her daughter could carry back. This time it was only a couple of items.

As she walked to the store that evening, the sun would be going down behind the trees in an hour or so. The young girl had walked those country roads all her life, and they were as familiar as the back of her hand. Never was she scared to walk alone to the general store, which was less than a mile from her home, even if it was getting dark. After all, when she was younger her guardian angel walked with her.

This day though, she had a dread of pending trouble. It

wasn't the feeling she had felt before — this was different. As she walked down the gravel road and was about half a mile from home, there was a bend in the road where on both sides grew blackberry bushes and tall Johnson grass. That's when there was a rustling of leaves coming from the right of her that she assumed was a rabbit looking for water, for it had been a hot day. Yet the sound was louder than a small animal would make, so she picked up speed from a stroll to long strides. Before she knew it she was running full speed ahead.

Elizabeth made it to the store all out of breath, and Mr. Jones asked her why she had been running on such a hot day. She was too embarrassed to explain to him that a rabbit had scared her or to admit she was afraid.

It was about closing time by now, but Elizabeth took her time looking around and pretending she had forgotten what her mother wanted her to pick up. Mr. Jones had already sliced off the pound of bologna and had wrapped it in the usual brown paper he tore off the huge roll next to the meat slicer.

Mr. Jones was getting impatient and asked if he could help her find something because by that time she had been there at least twenty minutes.

"Oh! I remember now. Its instant coffee my mama wanted," Elizabeth said, as she picked up a small jar of Maxwell House and set it on the counter next to the bologna. She told him that her mama said to put it on her credit account.

Mr. Jones looked even more out of sorts, and mumbled something to the effect, "I need to get a payment toward what your family owes me! " as he plopped the bag down on the counter with a thump.

She never told her mama what Mr. Jones had said, for she had already mentioned to her that they had to get some money to pay Mr. Jones.

She left the store without getting some toiletries her mother told her she could get for her birthday.

Heading back home in the dark with her little paper bag in hand, and still upset over Mr. Jones's hateful remark, she had all but forgotten about the sounds she had heard coming from the bushes earlier. As she approached the bend in the road, it was pitch dark and Elizabeth picked up her speed. Then out of the darkness something grabbed her, putting a sweaty hairy hand over her mouth. She heard heavy breathing, but couldn't make out who or what it was attacking her from behind. She couldn't breathe because the big hands had not only covered her mouth but her nostrils as well. But she kicked with all her might, dropping the grocery bag in her struggle. She heard a glass breaking. Even with all the fighting back she was doing, in the back of her mind she worried about her mama's coffee. Finally, she fell to the ground and when she did, she gasped for air and while trying to catch herself, her arms spread out with her right hand hitting something sharp like a stone or a piece of glass. She clutched it tight and came back as hard as she could hitting at the shadow in the dark. With a grunt and cursing, he ran off — not into the bushes but down the road toward Mr. Jones's grocery store.

When Elizabeth got home, she was still holding what she knew now to be a stone, as if it were glued to her hand. But she had lost the grocery bag.

Her mother met her as she came through the kitchen door. She had a worried look on her face. "Elizabeth, what has taken you so long? I was worried to death!" That's when she saw her daughter's knees, scrapped and bleeding. "What on earth has happened to you?" she asked with a shaking voice.

"I lost it, Mama," was all she could get out. Then she started crying uncontrollably, so much so it took a while to tell her mother what had happened to her. When she finally did get it all out, she could see the terrified look on her mother's face.

"Mama, I am so sorry I lost your groceries. I will go back down the road and look for them in the morning."

Maybe the jar had not broken, she thought.

"No, you are not ever walking down that road alone again! I will go with you the next time."

Elizabeth was sure her mother didn't have her coffee for a week or so after that, because neither she nor Elizabeth dared to walk down that road for a while.

Elizabeth's mother didn't tell her daughter that night, that while she was gone to the store, she had heard on the radio about a couple of escaped convicts who had been seen in the next county over, and everyone needed to keep an eye out for them for they could be dangerous.

As Elizabeth lay in bed that night, she wondered why her guardian angel hadn't warned her about the danger ahead. She remembered the uneasy feeling she had all day, but nothing bad happened as it always did when she had a sense of pending dread. Her guardian angel was always there protecting her.

The rock was lying on the floor at the end of her bed the next morning. She didn't remember even dropping it there. Looking closer she saw blood on the jagged edge where she must have hit the thing that attacked her, but she saw something more as she examined it closer. She saw that her fingers fit perfectly between the sharp edges of the rock, and as she slowly turned it around, there before her eyes was the exact shape of an angel — wings and all.

It wasn't by chance that in total darkness Elizabeth's

hand fell on that rock. Her guardian angel had been there all the while. It was she who hadn't believed or looked closely for her guidance as she once did as a child.

The police took the rock as evidence with them after the incident was reported, but only for a while. They returned it to her a few weeks later, after they captured the escaped convicts. She found out later the man who she hit with the rock had a gash the shape of a halo right in the middle of his forehead.

The police asked Elizabeth's mother if she had seen the attack, of course, she told them she hadn't. They explained to her why they asked her if she was there.

The person that attacked Elizabeth told the police he saw a woman in a long dress come out of nowhere, which is the reason he ran away. He told them he was distracted by the woman when the girl hit him with something. The police said that whoever came along most likely saved the girls life, for a cut no worse than the one he had, would not have stopped him from doing something awful to Elizabeth. She found out later that the man was a convicted murderer and a rapist.

The convict did go to the grocery store after he was scared off. Lucky for Mr. Jones, he had already locked up as soon as Elizabeth had left. The only damage done was the back door was broken along with some food taken.

Maybe Mr. Jones had his own angel. Elizabeth didn't know for sure, but she believed he thought it was a miracle he had closed the store when he had. Either way, he was a much nicer person after that.

Elizabeth still has the angel rock, even though it is only a rock it is a reminder to her that her real angel has always been there, and she suspects she will be for many more years to come.

The End

Getting Old

I see an old woman creeping up on me,
For every day a new wrinkle I see.
The bags are getting worse under my eyes,
From sleepless nights and constant sighs.

My hearing is not what it used to be,
And now the fine print I can no longer see.
For a long time my hair has been gray,
But a blonde I am and a blonde I'll stay.

There are a lot of things a woman can do,
Like a facelift and a tummy tuck too.
But I've seen some of these go terribly wrong,
There were no more wrinkles but the expression gone.

So I'll do what I can to keep the old woman away,
Put my makeup on and cover the gray.
Occasionally I may have a glass of wine,
And tip my glass to father time.

Mary Joyce Lawhorn

Dream Traveler

If I could start over what would I do?
Would I change a thing or two?
There were roads I wanted to go down,
But I was scared and turned around.

Never leaving but wanting to,
So my dreams would have to do.
I went to places far away,
And for a while there I would stay.

No one knew I was even gone,
For I was there all along.
Few could have gone where I've been,
And in a second be back again.

For only in my dreams did I travel far,
To be an artist or a movie star.
I once was a pilot, soaring high,
Clipping my wings against the sky.

I survived a storm in the open sea,
When a wave to the shore carried me.
Deep in Africa I stayed for a year,
And slept with the lions without any fear.

A Field Were Memories Grow

Even the Tiger ate out of my hand,
And like the beast I lived off the land.
No one believes I went to these places,
Nor that I have worn so many faces.

Who knows where the next place I will go,
Maybe cross the desert or to the North Pole.
Wherever it is that I'm destined to be,
I will dream a dream and it will take me.

I Am Not A Rat!

Ralph lives in New York City. His home is under a trash bin where he has lived all his life. His grandfather dug the hole single handed over thirty years ago.

Of course, a few things have changed — such as an extra hole was dug out to make room for the expanding family. The walls are lined with all sorts of things, such as fur, walnut hulls, and about anything you can imagine. All the furniture is made from scraps the family had carried from surrounding garbage dumps, and all in all it is quiet cozy.

Now Ralph is a big, brown rat — but don't tell him I said he was a rat —because to him that is the lowest form of species on the planet. I guess you could say Ralph is right about that, I don't know too many folks that like rats. Do you?

So each time Ralph goes out in public he will try to disguise himself. He hates it when folks scream, "EEK, there is a big ole rat!" He learned early on that no one screamed when they saw a kitty or a little dog.

Ralph knows he will never be a cute and cuddly pet for anyone, and he knows it is a tough life for rats, because no one leaves food out for them, or brings them in from the cold. In fact, it's right the other way around. People try to catch them in traps, bated with a nice piece of cheese, and for sure they don't want them in their homes.

There were many times he barely escaped with his life, trying to salvage something to eat for him and his family.

Once a butcher came out of his shop to dump scraps (there were always lots and lots of tasty scraps there) and Ralph was watching and waiting for his share first, before the greedy little mice in the community devoured them all.

One night the butcher came out carrying a garbage bag in one hand and in the other was a long, silver butcher knife. He had seen the "big ole rat" waiting out there several times before, and he had even set a trap once. But Ralph was too smart for that — after all he was a street-smart rat.

This time the butcher, with swift precision, came down with his knife. But the accuracy was detoured when the blade caught the tip of the butcher's hat and missed Ralph by half an inch or less. That's when he decided from now on when he went out, he would disguise himself.

Tonight Ralph was going to be a business man. No one would notice a man dressed in a suit! He would pretend he was outside getting some fresh air. "FRESH AIR! BY THE GARBAGE CAN????"

Now I didn't say Ralph was "book smart," I said he was street smart —there is a difference, you know!

It worked, not one person notices the business man, and not even the butcher seemed to pay any attention when he dumped the garbage. Ralph waited until he went back in the shop, then he quickly loaded his brief case down with fine meat and vegetables, even a hunk of cheddar cheese.

But, the butcher out-smarted Ralph once again. Before he could get away, around the corner came a policeman blowing his whistle, and holding a bobby stick in the air ready to clobber the big rat. Ralph took off in a flash. As he ran, his top hat blew off first. The next to fly off was his coat. Poor Ralph, all he could manage to do was hang on to his brief case full of food. Of course, his tie was still around his neck. Again, fate was on his side. Just as the cop was ready to nab him, he scurried under the garbage bin shaken, but safe from certain death if the policeman had hit him with that night-stick.

Needless to say Ralph stayed home for the rest of the night, but at least there was plenty of food for the family to munch on.

Every once in a while, he peeked out to see if there was any sign of the policeman around, but all he saw was lines of nasty little mice going back and forth to the garbage can, carrying what they could with their smelly, but sharp little teeth.

"Ugh! Nasty mice," he would mumble under his breath. Ralph hated mice.

During the night he heard a loud thud. It was the garbage truck again. He never got used to the noise of the big trucks lifting the bin from over him. It would come down with another bang as they put it back down over Ralph's hole to be filled up again. Of course, he was safe down under the ground in his rat hole — Sorry! Ralph's home.

A few months later he had another close call. Ralph was chatting with one of his buddies on top of the garbage bin, when all of a sudden they were being lifted high in the air by the big truck. Neither one had heard the truck drive up, so they were scrambling to find a way to jump off the bin. His friend made a daring leap and made it off. But it was too late for poor Ralph, and he was dumped into the truck and down came tons of garbage on top of him. Lucky for Ralph, a crate landed on top of him, protecting him from the falling junk.

The truck started moving and he had no idea where it was going. He was shaking from fright for, he had never been anywhere outside the city.

It seemed forever before the truck came to a stop, and then he heard the lever being raised to dump Ralph and all the garbage on top of him. It wasn't long before he could see the sky, but only for a fleeting second, and SWISHHHH, he and the crate went falling through the air landing on an old mattress.

He waited for a while until the truck was out of hearing range, and then he crawled from under a newspaper. Ralph looked around at miles and miles of old sofas, appliances, and hundreds of rusty tin cans.

"This must be where the rich folks live." He thought about a place his grandfather had told him about. He once told him that rats grew as big as dogs there at the land fill — big, fat and mean! Poor Ralph was shaking all over.

He backed under the newspaper and stayed until he stopped shaking, then he peeped out again. There was something going on a few feet from where he was. A huge, white animal was slapping a smaller animal. As he got a better look, he could see it wasn't just any animal, they were the biggest rats that he had ever seen. The white rat took a piece of bread from the smaller one and slapped him again.

I have got to get out of here! Ralph was thinking.

He was still scratching his head, trying to figure out his situation, when a Little Mouse crept up behind him. "You are new here, aren't you mister." She said in a squeaky little voice.

Back in the city it was unheard of for a mouse to speak to a rat because they were an even lower species than rats as far as Ralph was concerned, and the mice were usually scared of the bigger rodents.

This Little Mouse didn't seem to be afraid at all. After

all, this rat was a baby compared to what she had seen here at this dump. She asked Ralph if he was lost and he told her he had gotten trapped in a garbage bin and carried off.

"Oh, that has happened more times than you can imagine!" The Little Mouse told him.

"How do I get back home?" Ralph asked, trying to not act scared.

"Most of the time no one goes back. Usually the big rats here won't let them eat and they starve," she said with big, scared eyes, and she shook her head in defeat.

Ralph started shaking again and excused himself, telling Little Mouse he was cold as he ran under the paper again.

Unbeknown to Ralph, Little Mouse saw a way out of the terrible place she had been living most of her life, so she made Ralph a deal. She told him she could get him out if he would take her with him. Little Mouse said she had a rough life there, since she was accidently thrown away when she was only a baby. She couldn't remember much of the first few months, except trying to find small crumbs to live on. But when she grew up, she would listen to some of the stories the other mice told her about the city. She heard it was safer there and always plenty of food. But the best part she said was that no big rats lived there.

"Well, no bigger than me!" Ralph said, holding in his stomach to inflate his chest.

Even doing that, Little Mouse said he was still half the size of rats that live in the landfill.

"I will be safe there," she said, breathing a sigh of relief."

At that, Ralph let his belly fall and his shoulders drop — his ego deflated.

A Field Were Memories Grow

He accepted Little Mouse's offer. He would take her with him if she could get him out safe and sound. So they shook on the deal, and Little Mouse scurried away to pack up a few things to take with her. Waving goodbye, she said she would be in touch.

The next night, Little Mouse showed up where she last saw Ralph. She had a handkerchief tied to a stick full of her meager belongings. Ralph crawled out from under his newspaper and looked around, and then he reared up on his hind legs and started sniffing. All seemed to be safe enough, so he asked Little Mouse what her plan was.

"Just follow me, but we must hurry for the garbage truck will be here anytime." Her plan was, as soon as the garbage was dumped, they would jump on the back before the bed was lifted back up.

"Why haven't you tried this before?" Ralph asked.

"Because I can't jump high enough. I did try, but each time I hit the side of the truck bed and bounced off. What I want you to do is let me hold on to your tail when you jump. I think that will work, don't you, Ralph?"

"Well, you had better hang on tight, because that is a pretty high leap, even for a rat — I mean me," Ralph stammered.

Little Mouse knew the garbage truck always arrived on time, and she told Ralph he only had this one chance, because as soon as the big rats heard the truck drive away, they would all race there to see who would get the best portions.

"I have seen some really bad fights between them!" she whispered to Ralph. That was a lot of pressure Little Mouse was putting on Ralph.

Little Mouse was already holding on to Ralph's tail when the garbage came tumbling down. When the last bit hit the ground, Ralph made a running leap with Little

Mouse flying through the air, holding on to his tail with all her might. Her claws were slipping loose from Ralph's long slick tail, but she had just enough time to grab on to a patch of hair on Ralph's back before they hit the floor of the truck. She was literally hanging by a hair. Lucky for her it was very course and strong hair.

Ralph and Little Mouse made it to the city. All his friends were there to welcome him back. Not only was he safe, but he was hailed a hero for saving Little Mouse, whom just so happened to be of mice royalty.

They had a celebration for both rats and mice for the first time and there after they all lived in peace and harmony.

The End

A Field Were Memories Grow

Green Apples for Big Red

Big Red loved apples almost as much as Jan did, so each day they would see who would get to the apple tree first where big green apples hung by the bushel. Some would fall where it was easy for Big Red to get, but at the top the most delicious apples hung.

It was a game of sorts between the two that started the summer Big Red moved next door. Jan was used to having the apples all to herself — although she didn't mind sharing with her new neighbor. But the problem was, Big Red was really a mean bull and didn't want anyone on his side of the fence.

The tree really didn't belong to either of them, but a farmer up the road had rented the land to Big Red's owner. The huge red bull wasn't about to let the little girl have his apples — they were HIS now. Jan nicknamed him Big Red.

So early each morning when the dew was still glistening on the fields, and covering the apples like jewels, Jan would slip over the fence, while at the same time, keeping an eye out for the greedy bull. Those apples were the tastiest when plucked that early in the day.

Most of the time, Jan was first to get there. She would climb the tree and sit on a limb dangling her legs while taking in the early morning sun coming over the hill and enjoying a crisp, green apple. She would try to be down and across the field by the time Big Red came out of the barn walking slowly to his apple tree. Then about half way across the field, he would walk a little faster and flex his muscles to intimidate Jan if he saw her near the tree, and every once in a while, he would snort really loud.

This day, like a few other times, Jan didn't get down in time because she was daydreaming. So when she heard him snort, she knew he was too close to jump down and run, and he was headed straight for the apple tree.

Maybe he won't see me and when he gets his fill he will move on over to the woods where it was always cool, Jan thought.

But that was not going to happen. He looked straight up to where Jan was sitting and started digging in his front feet and snorting louder than she had ever heard him. She just knew he was going to charge the tree, which horrified Jan, because if he rammed that tree, it would fall and she would come tumbling down too. Then he stopped and looked up again at her with blood shot eyes and foam dripping from his mouth.

Jan threw the apple she was eating down to distract him, but he didn't even notice it. Instead, he decided to lay down under the shade of the apple tree.

Now what? Jan thought. *He is going to sleep and there is no telling how long I will have to be stuck up here.*

So she decided to throw an apple, but missed his head by a foot. Then she shook the tree as hard as she could. Even with apples falling on and around him, the bull would just slap his tale around as if swatting flies.

Nothing was working. Poor Jan even called her mother, but she couldn't hear her because she was too far away. The girl was all alone and would have to wait it out, and with any luck, sooner or later her big brother would surely come looking for her.

Jan had no idea what time it was, though it seemed

like hours since she climbed up that tree, and the stubborn bull was still asleep. Then she saw some hornets swarming around the half eaten apple she had thrown earlier at Big Red.

If I could stir them up, maybe they will land on the bull, Jan thought.

She aimed an apple and hit dead on where the hornets were buzzing around, and they flew off only to fly right back to that juicy apple. After that, hundreds of hornets joined in and soon she couldn't even see the apple until they flew off leaving only the core.

Big Red was still asleep and full of all the apples he had eaten. The hornets smelled the scent of apple juice on his face and hundreds of them landed on his nose. With a jerk and a snort the red bull jumped to his feet swatting the hornets as fast as he could with his tail.

Jan had never seen that bull run as fast as he did that day. With the hornets right behind him, he ran across the field in record time and into a pond to ease the stings that she was sure he had all over his nose.

After that day, Big Red wasn't as greedy. He would wait until Jan got her apples and then he would saunter on up and have a few for himself. Jan would sometimes pull the biggest apples off and leave them on the ground, knowing the best ones had always been out of reach for him. After all, she had been greedy too by not sharing with Big Red some of the best apples from the top.

The End

True Love

Like silk on wool they are so far apart,
But yet they are connected heart to heart.
He likes to go fishing and she stays at home,
And does the cleaning while he is gone.

She loves to shop but he hates the mall,
So he stays home and watches football.
Nothing in common between the two,
Except their love that is forever true.

When you see one the other isn't around,
Yet their love is solid and sound.
Just two people going their separate way,
But always together at the end of the day.

It's Hot Outside

Outside no birds are flying around,
All day I haven't heard a sound.

Because it's so hot the grass has died,
And what once was green is now brown and dried.

The tomatoes are cooking on the vine,
From lack of rain and too much sunshine.

I have hidden my ferns under the tree,
Instead of on the porch where they used to be.

The farmers are worried about what to do,
To save the crops and the animals too.

It's too hot to go outside,
So like my ferns I too will hide.

Pesky Pests

Creepy crawly little things,
Slimy, hairy and some with wings.
Long legs and stingers too,
Black, yellow, brown and sometimes blue.
Buzzing around or flying high,
Bumble bees and a dragon fly.
An army of ants in a row,
Day and night they are on the go.
Weaving webs to snare its prey,
A spider has food for another day.
A chigger hiding in the weeds,
Latching to skin on which it feeds.
Then a flea will bite the dog,
Making him jump like a frog.

A Field Were Memories Grow

Nature's Music

Peace is walking through the woods alone,
With the sound of nature tagging along.
Winding in and out of the trees,
Is the whisper of a summer breeze.

Drinking water from a spring so clear,
Resting on the bank so you can hear.
The peaceful sound of a rippling brook,
That can only be found in nature's book.

Are You Asleep Mama?

"Mama! Are you asleep?"

"No, Mary, but you should be!" Mary's mother answered back. Nancy was used to her daughter asking that same thing every night, and she knew what she would say next.

"Don't go to sleep until I do, Mama"

"I won't, now hush! So we both can sleep," Nancy said with a yawn.

For a year or longer, Mary would ask that same thing every night. Nancy didn't know why — maybe it was a phase all eight year olds went through.

Mary was her youngest daughter, and the two older children never seemed scared at that age. It worried Nancy — maybe she needed to talk to a doctor or read up on the problem.

Mary had put a buckeye under her pillow that night. She was told that if she would do that an elf would come and get it and leave money for her. The longer she lay there the more frightened she became. For in her mind, she imagined a little old elf with a pointed hat and pointed beard and even pointed ears walking across her belly to get to the pillow. She didn't want anything like that on her bed, so she threw the buckeye across the room. That's when she asked her mother if she was asleep. Things such as this caused her anxiety even if she did love to imagine off the wall things.

A Field Were Memories Grow

Mary knew she had a vivid imagination. The only thing was she didn't know if what she thought was real or not. But as long as she could remember, she believed there were really little fairies that lived in the woods, and they had little homes and little towns just like people do. She just knew they danced around the toad stools every night in their clothes made out of leaves and scraps of old cloth they found here and there. She knew also that they were always happy and singing in their own little world.

Mary tried to slip up on them because she wanted so much for them to be her friend. She would take food and little things out to where the toad stools were and leave them. She had even left notes asking if she could join them some night. Mary never got an answer, but that was because they more than likely didn't speak the same language as she did — at least that's what she figured.

Years passed and so did the phase of asking her mama if she was asleep every night. Of course, now she had her own room and was in high school.

Her family and friends would all make fun of her now if she even mentioned believing in fairy tales, so she quit talking about them. But that didn't stop her imagination from running wild, putting all her stories on paper and she even drew what she thought the fairies looked like. So by the time she graduated from high school, Mary had hundreds of illustrated manuscripts she had saved over the years and only she had seen them.

Mary's parents wanted her to go to college and get into something that she could make a career of. To their disappointment, she wanted to major in art and literature. Her goal was to write children books, also the illustrations would be the characters she knew all by name. Her mother wasn't all that surprised at her choice for she had seen this coming for years.

Mary's first children's book was published during her last year of college. I Live Under a Toad Stool, was top of the best seller list for three weeks, but this was only the beginning.

Mary is known worldwide. She has accomplished many things in her career. Not only has she sold more children books than any author in history, but has made hundreds of films based on her books. She traveled extensively throughout the world encouraging children to write about their dreams, fears and what they love.

"Mama, are you asleep?" Mary asked as she held her mother's hand, praying to hear her reassuring voice once more. But only silence filled the room as she whispered, "Mama, please don't go to sleep before I do.

The End

"Abby's Two Worlds"

Two sisters tell their story

Abby's Story

I am forty-five years old and will be entering into a life of which I do not know what to expect, nor will I remember the life I have had and cherished up until now. Already I forget my children's names at the most awkward moments, such as someone will ask, "How many children do you have, Mrs. Abby?"

I have to think and try to remember what my eldest son's name is so that I can count down to the youngest. "Four," I say, but Troy is not the oldest, then I remember, "Oh! I have five," correcting myself.

Some days are better than others, and on those good days I am in denial that I am slowly but surely passing from the life as I know it now. I get scared thinking about it, for I have such good memories of growing up with a house full of siblings.

I think of my mother, yes it makes me so sad that I will forget her and the person she was. The love she gave us kids was unconditional, and my children, I won't even know them when they call me Mama. I don't know what kind of person I will be then, though I get some idea on my bad days. I become very contrary and moody, yet the burden of loving is gone. I am alone, even from myself.

Once in a while, I see far back someplace, a young

man coming to meet me and we go for a walk through the woods, down a path covered with autumn leaves. I miss him, but I don't remember who he was or where he went. I just know that during those memories, I feel youth running through my body with only the feeling someone young can feel — and unblemished skin, smooth without wrinkles, even when I smile. I look forward to going back to that place in my mind. Maybe I will stay the next time.

Several people came by today. They all seemed happy to see me and told me that I was looking rested and well. I seemed to know some of them, especially the younger ones. I think Tabby is my daughter, but she called me nanny. Anyway, I pretended I knew exactly who she was and hugged her.

I don't like this place where I am living now because it's not familiar to me — yet I can't seem to remember where I lived before. I am confused — I stay so confused.

Tammy's Story

I hate having to come here to see my sister, but this is where she will stay from now on — among strangers, yet we are all strangers to her. So I guess I can take consolation in knowing it doesn't make any difference at this stage of her dementia. It's the ones that love her that hurts so much, having our sister right beside us, either looking straight ahead or staring at something that only she can see.

Abby left us all — where her world was full of life, love and so very smart. My sister doesn't know who I am anymore. I can tell because she looks at me with dark empty eyes. I think sometimes she is afraid of me, because she hides her things under her pillow when I walk in. She thinks I don't see and it reminds me of a very small child, slipping a cookie when she thinks no one is looking. How I miss my sister and best friend — the one whom I shared everything with.

I try to make small conversation with Abby, hoping deep in there she does hear me and knows why I am here. I do her nails and fix her hair, while all the time I talk to her about the fun we once had, and she will every now and then have a familiar gleam in her eyes. When I am through with her nails, she will look at her hands for the longest time, as if they are foreign to her. Once she looked at me with eyes as clear and bright as they used to be and said, "I remember you, Tammy," as she reached out to hug me. Those are the times that keep me going, even if it's a second that she is back, it is worth the pain of waiting and missing her.

Little by little my visits are growing fewer. I know I should go visit her, but it is too painful seeing her sit at the table strapped in and wearing a bib while someone feeds her. But they take good care of her — I am thankful for that.

"Mrs. Abby, come let's go to your room now." The care givers will say.

With her head down, she waits to be pushed back to that little room, no longer the proud beautiful woman that took so much pride in all she did.

The doctor said she could talk if she wanted to, at least say a few words because the nurses have heard her read out loud when no one is around. Maybe it is because she was a school teacher that she can still read. Like the older man up the hall from Abby, the one who sits every night going over his papers, he was once an accountant. Or the 90 year old war veteran across the hall that is still fighting his war. We know, because any given day you might hear the old soldier shouting out commands to his troops.

Tammy had seen how Alzheimer can destroy a family. She saw Abby's children grieve for five years, for there was no closure for them. She also knew the burden it puts on families that she had meet at the nursing home, and as much as they all loved Abby, it was no longer her. Her younger sister had slipped into another place sometime during the five years. No one saw her leave, for it didn't happen overnight. It was a gradual decline until she was gone from the world she once knew.

Tammy had made a decision. In the event that this awful disease ever befalls her, she legally made arraignment to be sent across the country to live out the rest of her life. She knew the burden wouldn't fall on her children if she were that far away.

Abby slipped away on a cold winter night while the world was sleeping, and no one saw her final departure. Maybe the world she went to was a much better place than the one she left behind.

The End

A Field Were Memories Grow

Where All Good People Go

When the curtain falls
and I take my final bow,
I'll change into something other
than what I'm wearing now.

I will leave this life forever,
accepting a brand new roll,
Walking on a stage
made of the purest gold.

Does the king still reign
high upon his throne.
While angels kneel
praising him with song.

What's it like up there,
are the streets really gold,
Are there no more tears,
like we were told.

Are you free of pain
that crippled your body so.
Are you young again,
where all good people go.

Mary Joyce Lawhorn

Do you sit with mama
remembering days gone by.
Enjoying a beautiful garden
where there's no reason to cry.

Give my love to all the ones
that I used to know,
That made it to the place,
where all good people go.

A Field Were Memories Grow

Another Sound

Waiting for the other shoe to drop,
Maybe it will or maybe not.
So I will keep listening for the sound,
Of another crises coming down.

When it is over I'll draw a sigh,
Kiss my worries all goodbye.
Another day will roll around,
What's that I hear? Another sound.

Go away! You're not welcome here,
And take with you my last tear.
There's nothing left for you to steal,
And no peace here for you to kill.

You have tried your last time,
To break me down and take what's mine.
My feet are placed flat on the ground,
Holding fast against your sound.

Mary Joyce Lawhorn

Rain Storms

Storms are brewing in the distant sky,
You can see the lightening flashing high.

The thunder claps with anger hands,
Shattering clouds and flooding lands.

The waters rise as the rain comes down,
And the wind blows with a mighty sound.

But then, all the world is quiet,
When from the sky peeps a light.

The wind is calm, the thunder's gone,
And with the clouds the storm moved on.

Grandma

Tell me a story that I haven't heard,
Not one about a goose or a mocking bird.

I don't want to hear about another bear,
About their porridge or a broken chair.

I am tired of the pigs and the big bad wolf,
And about the princess I've heard enough.

Not one about an egg that fell off a wall,
Nor about the kings men, for I've heard them all.

Tell me a story about you as a kid,
The games you played and the things you did.

Mary Joyce Lawhorn

One Lion's Secret

A mighty roar echoes through the night,
The monkeys stop playing and the birds are quiet.

He roars again to make sure they have heard,
Enjoying his reign over beast and bird.

He will creep silently searching his prey,
A nice big meal to end his day.

He has a reputation of being mean,
And like all lions he too is a king.

But he has a secret he is bound to keep,
He is a vegetarian and won't eat meat.

So at night he roars where all can hear,
Putting the jungle in a mighty fear.

He eats the berries until the bush is bare,
Then slips through the night back to his lair.

Hearts

The heart is a funny thing,
Sometimes it cries, sometimes it will sing.
It hurts at times when we love too much,
But it leaps with joy at a lovers touch.

Broken hearts grieve for the longest time,
Searching for the pieces that are left behind.
But like all things it too will mend,
By feeding it with love, it will live again.

Mary Joyce Lawhorn

Changes

He was standing at a distance; it had been awhile,
Since he had been back where he lived as a child.
Looking around so much had changed,
All his memories had been rearranged.

Where the little store had once stood,
Were only ashes and piles of wood.
The fields were no longer oceans of wheat,
They were replaced with a town and a busy street.

The creek was murky and the pond was dry,
Someone had even taken the blue from the sky.
Tall building bellowing smoke had turned it gray,
Smog filled the air where the children used to play.

No one takes the time now to stop and say hello,
Its rush hour in the city, everyone is on the go.
His little town had vanished, swallowed up by greed,
Buried under the city like a rotting seed.

A Field Were Memories Grow

A Visit

The snow was falling and getting deep,
And the cabin was too cold for the family to sleep.

The logs were gone with no way to get more,
For the snow had piled high against the door.

Mom spread quilts across each bed,
And put wool hats on each little head.

The temperature kept falling until it was zero,
With no fire in the cabin that was covered with snow.

What are we to do! Mom cried with dismay,
We only have food for one more day.

There is no wood so we are going to freeze,
And she started to pray on bended knees.

My children are hungry and I fear we will die,
I pray this request you do not deny.

Then right before them an angel stood,
And beside the stove was a stack of wood.

The angel smiled and faded away,
As the mother unaware continued to pray.

You can stop praying her husband said,
We have wood now and the angel left bread.

Mary Joyce Lawhorn

Losing Game

Games people play is a childless thing,
Trying to get even and placing blame.
No one wins for it's a losing game,
Both are hurt and full of shame.
The love they had was thrown away,
Destroyed forever by the games people play.
Like a puff of wind it's blown away,
Another heart broken by the games we play.

A Field Were Memories Grow

Mother's Day

Today is the day out of the year,
To celebrate mothers both far and near.

We may visit or even send flowers,
And to find the right card, we may spend hours.

But all mothers want is to spend time with you,
Not the perfect card or something new.

Of course all the gifts are very nice,
But the most important things don't carry a price.

Mary Joyce Lawhorn

Rat Race!

There was once a rat
who loved a little mouse,
They were born and raised
in the same little house.

Everything was fine
until they were grown,
Then the rat was told
to leave the mouse alone.

Mama rat said,
she is not your kind,
A nice little rat
you will need to find.

Little mouse was told
you are above that race,
They are nasty and mean
and have an ugly face.

So little mouse was sent
to a boarding school,
Where she might learn
about her family rule.

Her friend the rat
stayed at home,
Missing little mouse
but life went on.

A Field Were Memories Grow

Time went by
and mother mouse fell ill,
She became very weak
and she lost her will.

One day the rat
heard a mournful cry,
"I need help"
he heard mother mouse cry.

I would help you
if I wasn't a rat,
But I know how
you feel about all that.

Please help me Mr. Rat
I am begging you,
Even though I've been mean
and such a fool.

I will get Dr. Mouse
to come right away,
If I run fast enough
I'll be back this day.

Before he left
he made sure she was warm,
Covering her with a quilt
that was tattered and torn.

Mary Joyce Lawhorn

He put a scarf
around his pointed nose,
And little wool socks
on his long skinny toes.

Down the road he ran
as fast as he could,
Across the snow covered ground
and through the woods.

Knocking on the door,
but Dr. Mouse said go away,
"I care for only mice,
no rats! I say!"

But its mother mouse
that needs you, not I,
I fear if you don't come
she will surely die.

The snow is so deep
I can't possibly get there,
Even without snow
it would take an hour.

I know said the rat,
I will carry you there,
"No way, said the Dr.
everyone will stare."

A Field Were Memories Grow

"But I can't let mother mouse die."
the Dr. said,
So up on the rats back
and out the door they fled.

It wasn't an easy ride
on the big old rat,
He bounced up and down
and was chased by a cat.
The rat was fast
and he knew his way around,
Through the tunnels
that ran under the ground

Finally they made it
to the kitchen door,
Dr. Mouse jumped off
and scurried across the floor.

The Rat was so cold
and tired he fell asleep,
Then awakened by little mouse
rubbing his feet.

"Mother is fine
and it's all because of you,
You are a hero to me
and the whole town too."

Mary Joyce Lawhorn

Mama mouse recovered
in just a few days,
And to Mr. Rat
she couldn't give enough praise.

"I am sorry Mr. Rat
I've judged you wrong,
Wrong about the rats
all along."

"I hope we all
can mend our ways,
And become one race
one of these days.

Taken for Granted

We take so much for granted with those we love,
    Rarely taking the time to give them a hug.

Why is it though, if we are not sure love will stay,
We try so much harder, yet we give so much away.

Saying I love you comes easy, but it's rarely said,
Words go unspoken, thinking they know instead.

    If we tried as hard as we did so long ago,
Back when love was new it would never grow old.

Mary Joyce Lawhorn

Paradise Lost

The Lord made them a garden
as he gazed from afar,
And told them you are perfect
just the way you are.

He put them together
to grow in his garden place,
With a variety of shades
he created the perfect race.

"It is good" he said,
when he saw what he had made,
Man dwelling together
and with no one afraid.

In time sin did abound
and people hated each other,
Father turned against son
and a son against his mother.

The family in the garden
went on their separate ways,
The likeness of each moved on,
while the likeness of another stays.

Thus brought about a division
between all mankind,
That started out as one
in a garden lost in time.

Homeless

There is a picture in his pocket he carries all the time,
Cluttered with memories that's hard to find.
For his mind is foggy from all the whisky and wine,
Begging for a dollar- nickel or a dime.

He falls asleep on the street almost every night,
With a bottle of wine, holding it tight.
He pulls out the picture when there is no light,
For its too sad, so he keeps it out of sight.

He is getting old now and it's a matter of time
That he will be found with his bottle of wine.
They will look in his pocket for a name to find,
Then carry him away for the very last time.

A Spiders Web

Across the way hangs a silver string,
A sight to see and an awesome thing.
With a touch it will come tumbling down,
But a spider it will hold solid and sound.

The spider will use it for a trap to kill,
Holding it's prey like solid steel.
Nothing can escape the spider's snare,
He will devour its prey without a care.

Mr. Owl & Mr. Bat

The big old Owl said, "Hoo are you?"
"I'm Mr. Bat, how do you do?"

"I am fine, just hanging out,"
"Me too, and flying about."

"No one is out this time of night,
Most come out when its daylight."

"Who else do you see when hanging out?"
Mr. Owl thought; more bats no doubt.

"Oh I see other birds now and then,
Sometimes a fox coming out of her den."

"But us bats look so much like mice,
We are thought of as nasty and not very nice."

"So Mr. Owl why are you talking to me?
It's not something we often see."

"You know us owls think mice is a treat,
We swoop down and catch them with our beak.

"They are very tasty as a matter of fact."
He said, eyeing the bat for a midnight snack.

Mary Joyce Lawhorn

The Wonder of Life

I wonder where the bugs all go,
When it comes a freezing snow.

Do they go deep in the ground?
And wait for spring to come around.

Then what's the birds to do,
Since bugs are their favorite food?

Guess they scratch around for seeds,
That fell to the ground from dried up weeds.

Oh! but the world does go around,
Feeding all life from the fruitful ground.

Snow Covered Creek

The new fallen snow
lay silently across the way,
Where there used to be green pines
a white forest now lay.
The light of the moon
picked up the sparkling snow,
And it would light the way
to wherever we would go.

I would walk through the woods
just to watch the creek flow,
Running crystal clear
under the frozen ice and snow.
No other place
have I found to be so serene
As listening to water
run under a snow covered stream

Revised poem from; Changing winds of Autumn, 2005

Mary Joyce Lawhorn

Another's Shadow

The shadows are dark where in you abide,
You can't escape although you tried.
Never allowed to test your wings in flight,
For in the shadow there is no light.

Living in a shadow is a lonesome place,
You can't cast a shadow nor show your face.
Break away running and you will see,
Beyond the dark you are free.

A Field Were Memories Grow

The Old Barn

The barns tin roof echoed
as the rain fell outside,
While wrapped in a quilt
a little girl would hide.
She would go there
to be alone and dream,
Of the day she would become
a movie queen.

For hours she would rehearse
the scripts she would write,
While the rain made music
under the moons spotlight.
The stars all came out dancing
in their glittering gowns,
And the crickets with the frogs
made applauding sounds.

Then one day the stars
with the glittering gowns didn't show,
And the crickets went to bed early,
while the frogs lay low.
The little girl waited for hours
but no one came,
Even on the roof
there wasn't a drop of rain.

Mary Joyce Lawhorn

She would still go there
until she was about grown,
But some years later
the little girl moved on.
The old barn is still holding
her dreams inside,
And behind dark glasses
the stars still hide

Revised excerpt from:
A Field Where Memories Grow; 2003

A Trees Life

The trees are sad and so am I,
They are weeping though their leaves are dry.
Soon they will turn an awesome shade,
And under the leaves the children play.

The trees are sad and so am I,
For all living things will someday die.
Turning to dust they will blow away,
High on a mountain or a desert lay.

The trees are sad and so am I,
As to the autumn we say goodbye.
The fields are now covered with snow,
Where did all the colors go?

The trees are sad and so am I,
Shivering from the cold as winter crawls by.
But as sure as there is a tomorrow,
Happiness will replace yesterdays sorrow.

The trees are happy and so am I,
As the sun warms up the eastern sky.
Now the leaves are swaying to a joyful song,
While birds on the branches sing along.

Mary Joyce Lawhorn

A Happy Place

Come go with me for a little while,
And bring with you a happy smile.
Make my heart as good as new,
Mend the pieces that have broken into.

Take me to a peaceful place,
Where no perils we have to face.
No hateful words are spoken there,
Where burdens are light and easy to bear.

Where waters flow so pure and clear,
Cleansing our mind and bodies from fear.
Where cries of pain are never heard,
But only the songs of the mocking bird.

A Field Were Memories Grow

Only A Shoe

I am so low people walk on me,
And on the bottom I'll always be.
I have a tongue but I don't speak.
Some says at times I really reek.

Sometimes I am a heel and some say I'm flat,
And I can be a sneaker slipping up like a cat.
I have a lot of eyes but cannot see,
Because of laces they thread through me.

Some call me a loafer but I don't think I am.
Just because I'm always walking around.
I don't like it when it snows,
I'm stuffed with socks and nylon hose.

We are the same size and come in pairs,
Following each other up and down the stairs.
So when you see one you will see the other,
Standing side by side but never much further.

I travel many miles in just one day,
Sometimes at work or out to play.
I guess you could say I am shiny too,
At least I was when I was new.

Mary Joyce Lawhorn

I get kicked around because I'm tough,
Really I'm treated pretty rough.
Sometimes they use me for a swat,
Actually I am used quit a lot.

They slam me down on a fly,
Or step on a bug as it goes by.
Once a dog wet on me,
Instead of going behind a tree.

Then they put me through the mud,
In the snow and all kinds of crud.
Soon my sole wears so thin,
They throw me away or trade me in.

Tea Cup

I have a cup that was given to me,
A cup that was used to drink her tea.
The Gold is worn from around the lip,
Where hundreds of times she took a sip.

How many secrets was it told,
The beautiful cup she used to hold.
How many tears did it see fall,
While no one else saw them at all.

I'll put it away like I always do,
Filled with memories it has of you.
It's only a cup that's stained with tea,
A little cup that was given to me.

Mary Joyce Lawhorn

Trusting Heart

Maybe the heart is something more,
Like a window or an opened door.
Where love walks in for a little while,
And lingers on a lovers smile.

Maybe it closes its door from the pain,
To protect it from the tears that rain.
Then the sun will shine once more,
And the heart will open its trusting door.

Don't Let It Grow

Don't let anyone ruin your day,
By what they do or what they say.
Just shake it off and let it go,
Leave it alone don't let it grow.

Laugh away any sadness you feel,
For laughter helps your heart to heal.
You may not forget but try to forgive,
Where in your heart no grudges live.

For hate will eat up all that's good,
Leaving the heart as hard as wood.
And never again will it ever feel,
For a wooden heart can never heal.

Mary Joyce Lawhorn

Bugs, Slugs & Butterflies

I hate spiders,
I hate bugs,
I hate snakes
and I sure hate slugs.
I don't like flies
nor do I like fleas,
If they didn't sting
I would sort of like bees.

I like turtles,
frogs and butterflies,
And all the animals
in every size.
I love to watch
the birds fly high,
From the top of a tree
up to the sky.

I love the owl
because he is wise,
And the way he shuts
his big old eyes.
He sits up high
in a sycamore tree,
Hooting loud
at you and me.

A Field Were Memories Grow

Angry Storm

The thunder is mad and rumbling loud,
Throwing fire from the cloud.
Then the rain comes down hard.
Filling the creek and flooding the yard.

The trees are blowing from the wind,
Some will fall and all will bend.
The thunder still rolls but not as loud,
As the wind pushes away the angry cloud.

The sun will soon peep out to find,
All is clear so he can shine.
Then he will sleep for a while,
Waiting for the old moon to finally smile.

Mary Joyce Lawhorn

Old House

A little house between rolling hills,
Surrounded by trees and daffodils.
No one lived there anymore,
Like they did many years before.

I wanted to see what was inside,
The little house on a mountain side.
The door was ajar so I walked in,
Where for years no one had been.

The floor was made from chestnut wood,
And in the corner a rocking chair stood.
The house was musky and filled with gloom,
As I walked into another room.

A stove was still there and a coffee pot,
Still sitting there like someone forgot.
There was a table with a broken leg,
Put back together with a wooden peg.

Out in the back was a dug out well,
Where a dipper hung on a rusty nail.
A building had fallen into a heap,
Where chicks once lived now possums sleep.

A Field Were Memories Grow

There was a barn across the way,
That had seen its better day.
The roof was twisted and about gone,
From the winds that had blown.

The creek was still there and a fishing hole,
And an old man fishing with an old cane pole.
He remembered fishing there as a kid,
Just like he said his daddy did.

Mary Joyce Lawhorn

Her First Day Of School

The building looked so very tall,
To a little girl that was so small.
I am not afraid she smiled and said,
School is nothing for me to dread.

Stand up my child straight and tall,
Keep your pride in front of them all.
The little girl remembered well,
All the stories her mother would tell.

As she walked into school alone,
She turned and waved but her mother was gone.
But she had been there for her first day,
Like she promised before she went away.

A Field Were Memories Grow

When Men Were Free

There was a place where men were free,
And beauty as far as the eye could see.
Peace prevailed throughout the land,
For it was blessed by the makers hand.

All they had to do was care for this place,
And fill it with the human race.
Then they were tempted and believed a lie,
And because of this mankind would die.

So this beautiful place they had to leave,
For allowing evil to deceive.
Man would now work by the sweat of his brow,
And that's how it was and is until now.

Mary Joyce Lawhorn

Just the Way You Are

I am who I am and will not change,
Take me as I am, don't try to rearrange.
I may not be perfect nor will I ever be,
But I am the same as when you met me.

I would not change you even if I could,
I knew in the beginning I never would.
For you are perfect just the way you are,
And in your presence I will never tire.

Bad Seed

There is someone somewhere without a care,
Someplace in the world but I don't know where.
Then there are ones that are very sad,
Because their world is so bad.

A war that won't go away,
Not even for a single day.
People too scared to go outside,
Because of so many there have died.

From a bomb or a missile thrown,
Some little towns are completely gone.
Fighting is all they have ever known,
From the day they were born until they are grown.

They have never known a peaceful life,
In the middle of a war of sorrow and strife.
In the other world there is hate and greed,
Not given a thought of those in need.

Where riches and fame is their only goal,
Blinded by wealth they lose their soul.
Buy a new car and a mansion on a hill,
Sit down to a feast and have their fill.

Mary Joyce Lawhorn

Yet happiness eluded them making them sad,
Even with all the riches that they had.
Because money can't buy them one more day,
When on their death bed they finally lay.

So now we have a world with two sides,
Where all the rich and poor reside.
Hate is the same and so is the greed,
Because it all grows from the wicked seed.

My Empty Heart

I have always know from the very start,
That you were mine and I gave you my heart.
You held it tenderly for a long time,
Then you became careless and treated it unkind.

You left it lonely time and time again,
And I often wondered what could have been.
It cried out for you but you didn't hear,
And it would beat fast whenever you were near.

Then it stopped trying because love was gone,
Not feeling or believing but it beat on.
In time you remembered that you held my heart,
But love had died from the years apart.

I know you tried but you waited too long,
To take back the heart that you left alone.
So you walked away with your head bent low,
Leaving an empty heart that once loved you so.

Mary Joyce Lawhorn

A Battle Won

Cancer is a word we dread to hear,
That name alone causes so much fear.
We have seen so many with this disease,
With the pain and suffering that one sees.

It slips up without any warning,
Like a storm it was already forming.
A cloud hovers low for the longest time,
And bitter are we like pieces of brine.

But there is hope just up ahead,
From this cancer we tearfully dread.
For many survived and learned to cope,
Leaving another with strength and hope.

They are solders off to a war,
To fight a battle that was fought before.
Myriads of survivors against one foe,
Aiming straight with the arrow and bow.

A Field Were Memories Grow

Memories in a Bottle

If I could keep time in a bottle what would it hold,
   Would I keep memories there until I am old.
   Or would I fill it with hate so I could recall,
     All the bad times in life that I saw.

No! I would capture the happiest days of my life,
   Store it away from the sorrow and striff.
   And the bottle I would forever hold,
   Remembering the good until I grew old.

Mary Joyce Lawhorn

In Time

All she sees now is cold dark eyes,
From the cheating and constant lies.
Once they shined like the western sky,
With just a glimpse as she passed by.

But the storms of life became too much,
No longer did they speak or even touch.
He went his way and she stayed alone,
Hoping someday he would come home.

But in time she began to heal,
She was no longer numb, now she could feel.
She packed her things and went away,
Explaining nothing; she had nothing to say.

A year had gone by and she had a new life,
No longer lonely; no longer his wife.
Then he decided he would go home,
Only to find everything was gone.

Old Poets Never Die

Poetry written from another time,
Beautiful words but they aren't mine.
Poe wrote with a damaged mind,
But remembered for all time.
A genies he was way back then,
Proven the best that's ever been.
Others tried to fill his shoes,
And stealing his style they would often lose.
There were others that came along,
But like Poe they are gone.
Yet words lived on that they wrote,
And through the ages we still quote.
Even today they are still around,
Spewing words from the ground.

www.ingramcontent.com/pod-product-compliance
Lightning Source LLC
Chambersburg PA
CBHW071719040426
42446CB00011B/2133